ORKNEY DAYS

LUCY DOUGALL

PUGET SOUND PRESS
SEATTLE, WASHINGTON

ORKNEY DAYS

For information about permission to
reproduce selections from this book, write to:
Puget Sound Press
6523 California Ave. SW
PMB292
Seattle, WA 98136-1833
http://www.pugetsoundpress.com
lucy1925@aol.com
psp@pugetsoundpress.com

Art Work by Dixie Palmer Peaslee
Cover design by Dean Ingram

1 2 3 4 5 6 7 8 9 0

Heartfelt thanks to my good friends
Mary Ann Van der Muelen, who gave invaluable help in editing
Frances McCue, my mentor, who gave me the encouragement
to write poetry

and to the people and islands of Orkney, Scotland

For my children and grandchildren

CONTENTS

Cold Days in Scotland

A gale-force wind comes rocketing off the sea
tears the tops from waves and hits the farm
head-on, then skirls around the corners
shrieks through cracks with arctic breath.
Our house allows but one warm room
for refuge. The stone-cold home reminds us
it was always so. Each croft had one
heart-center, a crackling fire for warmth
and food, the leaping flames alive with stories
of wraiths and witches, kelpies, spunkies, ghosts.

Central heating is a leveling device —
all rooms are equal. Daughters and sons
retreat like snails
into their separate shells.

In a small croft in Alloway, the bard
of Scotland was born in a box-bed by the hearth,
steeped in his father's lessons, his mother's songs,
lulled by the nightly whisperings, rustlings
of straw, the snuffling munch of cattle
under the same roof. No privacy, you say.
But something else — I felt it – in our cold house
in Scotland within snorting distance of the byre.

The Old Man of Hoy

The walk starts gently enough
up the golden swale
leaving fen and bog
and scattered crofts below.

Then you meet the wind
head-on, and mist
rolling in on the sea,
and the keening cries of birds.

You are on the moor, the miles
of heather-covered hills, only this
between you and the sky.
You stop abruptly at the cliff edge

that drops a thousand feet
down to the sea, to waves
that pound and crush
the cliffs to shingle.

Rock and heather, springy and tough,
resilient through storms.
Do landscapes seep into the bones
and spirit of a people?

You wonder at that stab of recognition —
when a place unknown and yet familiar
mirrors a landscape
deep in a layer of your mind.

One pillar of pink rock: The Old Man
of Hoy, a sea-stack sentinel,
stands watch beside the cliffs.
One lonely sign near these dark moors:

There is no rescue here; climbers
proceed at their own risk.
And walkers, too, but theirs is a different
falling, a different finding.

Tomb of the Eagles

Just walk to the edge, he said,
where the cliff plunges to the sea.
You can't miss the mound.

A wind-lashed moor lies
drenched in salt and spirit voices.
Below the sea cliffs' jagged wall,
two restless seas collide to form
the stormy Pentland Firth —
whirlpools and racing tide
that rage above drowned ships.

On hands and knees we crawl
the dank stone passage, feeling
our way across 5,000 years.
Flashlight beams expose a huge
communal grave, rows of small
dark chambers built with slabs of stone.
Skulls stare from niches in the walls,
surrounded by scattered bones
of white-tailed eagles, majestic birds of prey
whose wingspan can exceed six feet
and lifespan 40 years —
old age for this prehistoric clan.

Back, blinking in the sunlight,
all land is sacred as we lie
dreaming in the heather,
listening to the crashing surf,
to the gulls that scream from the skerries.

Orkney Farmer

Fenced by barbed wire and standing stones,
sheep pastures fringe the shore.
We pass the laird's house on the rise —
stately, many-chimneyed, old. The dying sun
sets window panes ablaze as if inside
the chandeliers were lit for feasts and dancing.
The moment passes, leaving a dark silence
on the house and weathered roofless crofts,
all abandoned with a way of life. On modern
farms, the wind-tight byres and houses scoff
at storms; the farmer works as hard as any
crofter, but it is *his* farm, *his* chosen life.
When he plows up an ancient tomb, heedless
of archeology or any former steward's past,
he covers up his find and gets on with his work.

The Children at Dingieshowe

We heard them before we saw them —
shouts of wild joy
tidal waves of laughter
beyond the headland there they were
flying
leaping off the dunes like mad rabbits
turning cartwheels
flinging sand high
into the blue
shining air.

The Selkie

Our crunching steps alert
the sleek gray shape upon the beach.
She opens her soft eyes,

ruffles her fur, and slides
into the salty shallows by the shore
to disappear.

She surfaces far out
and in her mournful song
calls us from waters

of our birth in cries
below the ordering mind
half-human, plangent, wild.

Orkney Byre

A February night is all hot life inside the byre.
Some twenty cows stand munching, snuffling, twitching,
alert and patient, waiting for their time to calve.
We've kept one bull nearby to calm the cows, he said,
'twill seem more natural.

A pungent smell of silage stings the nostrils;
cow muck slaps down on ancient stony floors.
Dark-stained in random patterns oozing green,
the walls are like some modern mural
evoking dark memories of primeval time.

The TV camera stares down the row of cows,
its message relayed to the house.
Red barley sacks hang slack by bare
ceiling bulbs to block their glare.
In the corner, fresh straw gleams.

Warned by the screen beside his bed, the sleeping farmer
springs awake, dons oilskins and high boots
to cheat the horizontal rain and icy wind,
jumps in his white jeep, and speeds to the medieval byre.

He walks straight to the straining cow
and with a pitchfork lays a clean
and fragrant bed of straw beneath her.
With skillful hands he grabs the slippery legs
and eases a new life into the world.

If I could have my pick of all the earth's
sophisticated cities, towns of teeming traffic,
ordered lives from nine to five,
I would trade them all for one night of calving in my Orkney byre.

David

Daily life on his farm unrolled
outside our kitchen window: David,
swinging a shepherd's crook,
herding sheep up the road or
driving the green front-loader
from pasture to barn to byre,
a lone figure tramping
the cliff-edged fields
in search of a missing lamb.

He was part of the land —
of the long dark rows
that he ploughed, of the wide
fields and pastures facing
the cold North Sea.

Up before dawn, working late
into the night, he would still take time
from his rounds to help a neighbor
plant potatoes, or stop by our door
to offer help with gentle courtesy
or simply make us feel at home.
And his laughing eyes,
brilliant and blue as the sky,
enchanted us all.

He took us to Harvest Homes
and ceilidhs where we sat with
local families at long tables
heaped with scones and pots of tea.
One evening there, he rose
in answer to an inner prompting —
I'll just be checkin' the cows, he said,
left the dancing, drove to
the steamy byre where pungent
smells of silage clung to the dark
stony floors. He helped a cow
give birth, scrubbed clean his bloody
hands, and then returned
to dance the night away.

One blustery afternoon, he walked
with us above the cliffs through
salty wind whirring with guillemots,
then suddenly flung himself down and spread
his arms out in the fragrant heather,
took deep breaths of sun
and wind and earth, his land.

Our year's last morning,
the phone rang early
and in the lilting cadence
of his Orkney tongue
he told us that the sunrise
was especially fine, *Do ye not
want to see it on your last day?*

A year later, another phone call
broke the news.
They found him dead by the gate
he had been climbing over. The gun
he carried to scatter crows
or shoot rabbits misfired,
a shot that split the soundless air.

The road across the island
to the little graveyard by the sea
was blocked for miles. The church
could not contain the mourners.
It was a perfect day, his widow
kept repeating, *not a breath of wind.*
In Orkney where the wind blows
relentlessly, this rare cessation —
a sunlit stillness — marked
the stillness of another breath.

The Farm

Like a family, like a child, a farm
draws you into its vortex, whirls you
round in coils of needs. Neglect can kill.
Fields must be plowed, the harvest sown
and gathered, machinery tuned, fences
repaired, animals fed and cared for.

On a small island farm, a family
weathers the carnival of birth and death.
The father's cruel accident leaves mother,
daughter, son knit in communal harness.
The son comes into his own,
at home with his bright farm machines.
I've got the barley in! he sings
across the freshly planted fields.

In the byre at lambing time, the women
join in midwives' work, the mother's arm
plunged deep inside the womb, untangling twins,
her daughter holding fast the ewe. Another
birth, another life to care for. Mother
and daughter keep watch with radiant faces
as if the new life were their own.

Uncertainty is certain, like the weather.
None dares to drop the load, each one
a juggler balancing barbed wire bales.
An inner voice may shout for incarnation –
to paint, to write, to break out, to be free –
but each spring fields turn green
and winter's wind and mud and dark recede.

Ring of Brodgar

On our first visit we did not see the sign,
only the standing stones, each one austere
against the slate-blue sky.
We might have been alone upon the earth,
the only sound the moor-swept wind.
A cathedral as a structure stands alone,
but the standing stones are not
complete without the background
of the towering, changing sky.
In storms of driving rain and wind,
the stones loom powerful, enduring.

When the sky burns cobalt blue,
we lie in hollows sheltered from
the wind and have our picnic,
bread and wine, in this place
where the summer solstice
is a sacred moment of the year,
where on midsummer's dawn, we face
the Comet Stone and see the rising sun
bisect the purple heather sea
to arc above our heads
through its highest trajectory.
On days like these
we live outside of time.

Winter Gales

The wind blows down with unchecked fury from arctic wastes.
Stinging, lashing rain drives hard in horizontal streaks
across the grey-green sea, the grey-blue sky.

We cannot miss this chance to feel the wildness of the storm.
Wind-zippered and oil-skinned, we pull on boots
and spin out the door under full sail,
heading for the sea.
Chalk-white waves, churning sea foam,
climb high on the lonely beaches.
They crash in fragments on the skerries
and pour through crevices of rock-rimmed coves,
gorging them with spumy bubbles.
Roiling, savage surf pounds darkly against the looming cliffs,
shooting clouds of spray high
onto the deserted moor.

In the midst of this fierce turmoil, graceful fulmars,
northern seabirds, soar on updrafts from the cliffs
or ride the waves as though on a summer sea,
while on the moorland, sheep are more like us,
they stand close-huddled, backs to the wind.

In Winter I Look South

through rain-sluiced panes
to a moody sky
watching the shadowed sun
trace its lowering arc
on the far horizon.

Our slickered farmer butts
against the shrieking wind
and horizontal rain
that drums incessantly
on metal sheds and byres.
He walks aslant,
his head tucked down
and collar up, ignoring
or enduring
the relentless storm.

Then suddenly, the sun flares out,
an incandescent globe hung
in a clean-rinsed sky.
I can almost see the blue
return to his merry eyes.

That Great Orchestra

Mewing gulls, honking geese,
lowing cattle content
and meditative as the earth
or else brash and insistent
as the pungent silage, acid-sharp,
that stings my nose.
Staccato baas of sheep,
squawks of chickens, all tuned
to the keening wind
that plays an Aeolian harp,
the metal bars that string
our pasture gate.

Birdwatch

Eroded, layered precipices lean
above the sea — home to thousands
of birds — churring, soaring, hissing,
squabbling, vying for space
in skyscraper cliffs that teem
like tenements — spitting fulmars,
guillemots, kittiwakes, shags.
Others nest on the open moor. Fields
turn to feathered flying carpets
as we approach — oyster catchers
of the orange bills, lapwings, curlews.

Stout-shoed watchers flock to the island,
peer through binoculars, count and catalog
the birds, and then move on.

Birds, in Orkney, are front-page news:
Snow buntings sighted at Skara Brae —
A smew blows in to the Harray Loch —
Wintering whimbrels on Shapinsay.
Some are residents, some riders
on the highway of migration,
some rare visitors lost in fog or blown off-course.
Others are simple wanderers, like us,
who just chance by and are bewitched
and never leave this island refuge,
washed by the northern sea.

Three Ponies

Three ponies pause, wind-ruffled
on an empty moor. Small and sturdy,
they nuzzle the scratchy heather.
Above, black clouds churn
turbulent in the towering sky.
For miles the brackened land
lies sparse and bare.
Beside a lake of deepest indigo
a solitary croft stands empty,
low-built of grey native stone,
a hearth that once gave refuge
from the bitter winter storms
sweeping across these northern
isles in darkening days
when I feel most alone.
The ponies shelter in the hollows,
riding out the winter storms,
needing no fire, just their winter coats.

High-Heeled Sheep

Encased in fleece
on spindly legs,
they graze oblivious
to the cliff's edge
and waddle like plump dowagers
above the high-bluffed shore.

Suddenly, they reel seaward —
fluffy white bundles
tumbling, tumbling.
What sends them hurtling
toward the precipice?

Julian

People were a little doubtful,
not to say skeptical,
of this newcomer who
called himself a healer.
Then one mother,
who found no one
to help her on
the entire island,
made her way to his door
as a last resort.
Well, that was the start
of it. Next came the father,
then the seven children,
and finally, the cows.

Up-Helly-A

A Viking ship goes up in flames,
ignited by a hail of torches
tossed upon the dragon-headed galley
by rowdy Shetlanders at their great carnival.

The darkest hours of their northern winter
blaze with dance and song and fiery glow,
commemorating ancient voyages
when sacking, burning in a far-off land
were glorious deeds kept sacred in the sagas
passed down from chief to son in ringing verse.

So now this old excitement kindles
all-night revelry, Up-Helly-A.
The fierce, costumed squads come
from all the isles, each with a Viking chief.
They sally round the town from hall to hall
engaging all the company in dance and song
while good ladies serve them tea and crumpets.

Stones and Cows

You often see the cows and sheep
scratch their hides on the standing stones,
lie in their shade, or walk around
those ancient slabs where they feel at home.

What is this strange affinity?
a force and power we also feel,
but unlike us, they accept the gift.
The cows don't feel the need to explain.

Shape-Shifter Sky

1.

When winter skies lie heavy
on my land, I dream of Orkney
in the pathway of the storms
where swirling clouds roll in
forever from the sea.
And if I could
I would buy that sky
from witches who sell
good winds to sailors
for sixpence apiece.

2.

Sky-shafts of peacock blue and green flash by
like stained glass window colors cracked by light
and shattered into sharp and shining fragments
that fall to the darkened earth and stab the heart.

3.

The air hangs hot, oppressive, ominous;
distant thunder cracks and echoes;
the fields turn topaz in the sultry light.
Above the ruined mansion of old stone
the lowering clouds lie flat like slate.
Then the sky opens wide its sluice gates,
and warm summer rain spills down in sheets.

4.

Outside the croft I watch black clouds
float by on seas of fire like ships of Vikings
westbound, fleeing the ordered framework
they despise: farmhouse and steamy byres.

Their longboats crack the northern seas,
but sailors keep in their hearts
the fireside smell, the children's cries,
and when they land, it's not to loot and fight.

5.

I went from landscape where the sky
is backdrop for evergreens
and mountain peaks, to land
where sky is everything,
a huge inverted bowl of blue.
Rainbows and double rainbows
erupt like lava, then drop
over cliffs and sink into the bay.

Perspective shifts from vertical
to horizontal, sweeps like a pilot's
radar scope across the fields
and moor and sea opening
wider at each turn
to beyond the encircling sea
to what seems like infinity.

Merry Dancers

Have you ever seen the Merry Dancers?
Step outside the back door and look north.
From the far horizon to the zenith —
see the promise of an opening night
in an undulating satin curtain,
dazzling wide white streaks of winter light.

Intermittent flashes of rose-orange
set the canopy of sky ablaze;
electric green shafts pierce like icy arrows
through layers of your ordinary days.
One night is enough for all remembering.
Just step outside and gaze.

The Phone Call

An ordinary thing: I telephone a friend
across the ocean, a widow of three years.
A satellite beams back a voice, not hers,
but his. My heart turns over at the sound.
"That's grand you'll come," he says; and *"Aye, 'twill be
very busy come lambing time."* I see him
standing at the wall phone just inside
the gray stone farmhouse, laughing eyes
and face flushed by the sea-cliff's wind,
stamping his muddy boots fresh from the byre.
No frozen photograph could peel the scab
from the deep wound we thought had healed
as that voice did, the voice he gave his son,
and that his son, unknowingly, gave us.

And as we talked — I asked him questions
just to keep him talking — I heard a new
calm confidence. Sometimes it takes death
and fearful loss to catapult a son into
his rightful self, the one his father always
hoped for him but never lived to see.
He shoulders all his father left undone,
in his own way, and as I listen to his voice,
I know his father listens too.

Undercurrents

Last night I dreamed you came again
to stand at my kitchen door. You told me
that your sheep had strayed.   In asking
help, you gave. I felt a current flow
under the words and jump the gap
between our lives. You charmed us all
with your blue laughing eyes, made each
feel rare, like one choice stone upon
a beach of stones, linked
through you to all the rest.

Orkney Days

The North Sea splinters on rocks
like the hull of a Viking ship
spilling sagas on the sand.

Shadows of giants streak from
the standing stones when Northern
Lights whitewash the sky.

As the eyelid of sun sinks under
the horizon, a green flash glazes
the sea with emeralds. But drama

is not everything. Sheep graze
outside my window, lambing season
has begun, the birds are flying north.

Some of the poems in this book have won prizes in the
Scottish International Poetry Competition,
others have appeared in *Bellowing Ark.*

Other poems by the author have appeared in *The Lyric,*
Harp-Strings Poetry Journal, Amelia Magazine,
New Hope International Review and Positively Poetry,
an International Anthology of Little Press Poets.

ORKNEY ISLANDS ———

SCOTLAND ———

ABOUT THE AUTHOR:

Lucy Dougall has led an adventuring life with her husband, from hiking in the Arctic to mountain climbing in Africa, to sabbatical years spent in France, Australia, Chile, Kenya, and Nepal. Her life has been profoundly inspired by the natural world, unusual landscapes, and the people who inhabit them.

This book reflects a year spent in the Orkney Islands of northern Scotland. A deep connection to the land and people has led to yearly sojourns in these wild and windswept islands.